BUILDING BLOCKS OF GEOGRAPHY

CLIMATE AND BIOMES

Written by Izzi Howell

Illustrated by Steve Evans

WORLD BOOK

a Scott Fetzer company
Chicago

World Book, Inc.
180 North LaSalle Street
Suite 900
Chicago, Illinois 60601
USA

For information about other World Book publications,
visit our website at **www.worldbook.com**
or call **1-800-WORLDBK (967-5325)**.
For information about sales to schools and libraries,
call 1-800-975-3250 (United States),
or 1-800-837-5365 (Canada).

Library of Congress Cataloging-in-Publication Data
for this volume has been applied for.

Building Blocks of Geography
ISBN: 978-0-7166-4275-6 (set, hc.)

Climate and Biomes
ISBN: 978-0-7166-4277-0 (hc.)

Also available as:
ISBN: 978-0-7166-4287-9 (e-book)

1st printing June 2022

WORLD BOOK STAFF
Executive Committee
President: Geoff Broderick
Vice President, Editorial: Tom Evans
Vice President, Finance: Donald D. Keller
Vice President, Marketing: Jean Lin
Vice President, International: Eddy Kisman
Vice President, Technology: Jason Dole
Director, Human Resources: Bev Ecker

Editorial
Manager, New Content: Jeff De La Rosa
Associate Manager, New Product:
　Nicholas Kilzer
Sr. Editor: Shawn Brennan
Proofreader: Nathalie Strassheim

Graphics and Design
Sr. Visual Communications Designer:
　Melanie Bender
Sr. Web Designer/Digital Media Developer:
　Matt Carrington
Coordinator, Design Development:
　Brenda Tropinski

Acknowledgments:
Writer: Izzi Howell
Illustrator: Steve Evans
Series advisor: Marjorie Frank

Developed with World Book by
White-Thomson Publishing LTD
www.wtpub.co.uk

TABLE OF CONTENTS

There is a glossary on page 40. Terms defined in the glossary are in type **that looks like this** on their first appearance.

What a beautiful day!
Hey! I'm Climate!
You can thank me for the lovely sunshine that you usually find here on the savanna.

I'm not the same as weather, which changes from day to day, or even minute to minute!
Where's my umbrella?

Climate is the average weather in an area over a long period of time. Weather conditions are compared over years and years to find a pattern.
JAN 12
JUNE 2
SEPT 6
MAY 8
5
OCT 7
JULY 16
FEB 14
MAR 19
SEP 29
11
AUG 21

An area's climate is described in terms of temperature, variations in temperature, and amounts of sunshine ...

... kinds and amounts of precipitation (rain, snow, hail), levels of humidity, and frequency of storms ...

... and wind speed and direction.

Speaking of wind ... This is my friend, Wind!
Yes! I play a very important role in climates!

WHAT AFFECTS CLIMATE?

INFLUENCE 1

The area's **latitude,** or its distance from the **equator** towards one of Earth's poles. The equator has a latitude of 0°. The North Pole is 90° N latitude and the South Pole is 90° S latitude.

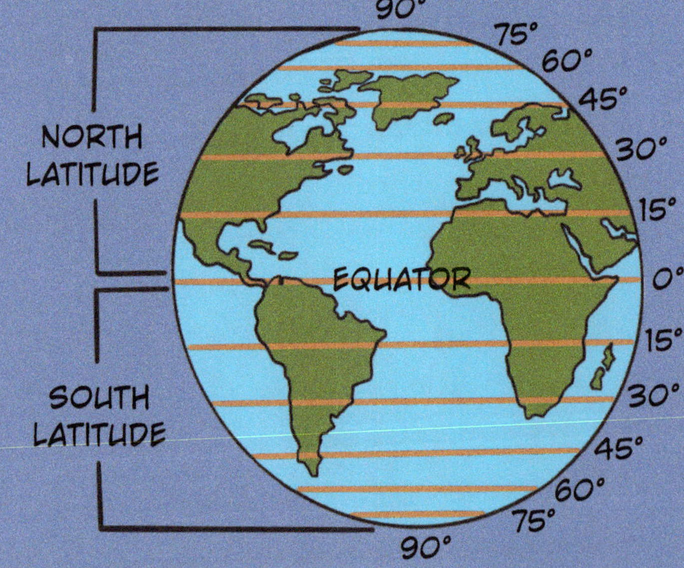

Closer to the equator, the sun's rays shine almost straight down upon the land. Such direct rays produce warmer temperatures. Parts of the globe farther from the equator curve away from the sun.

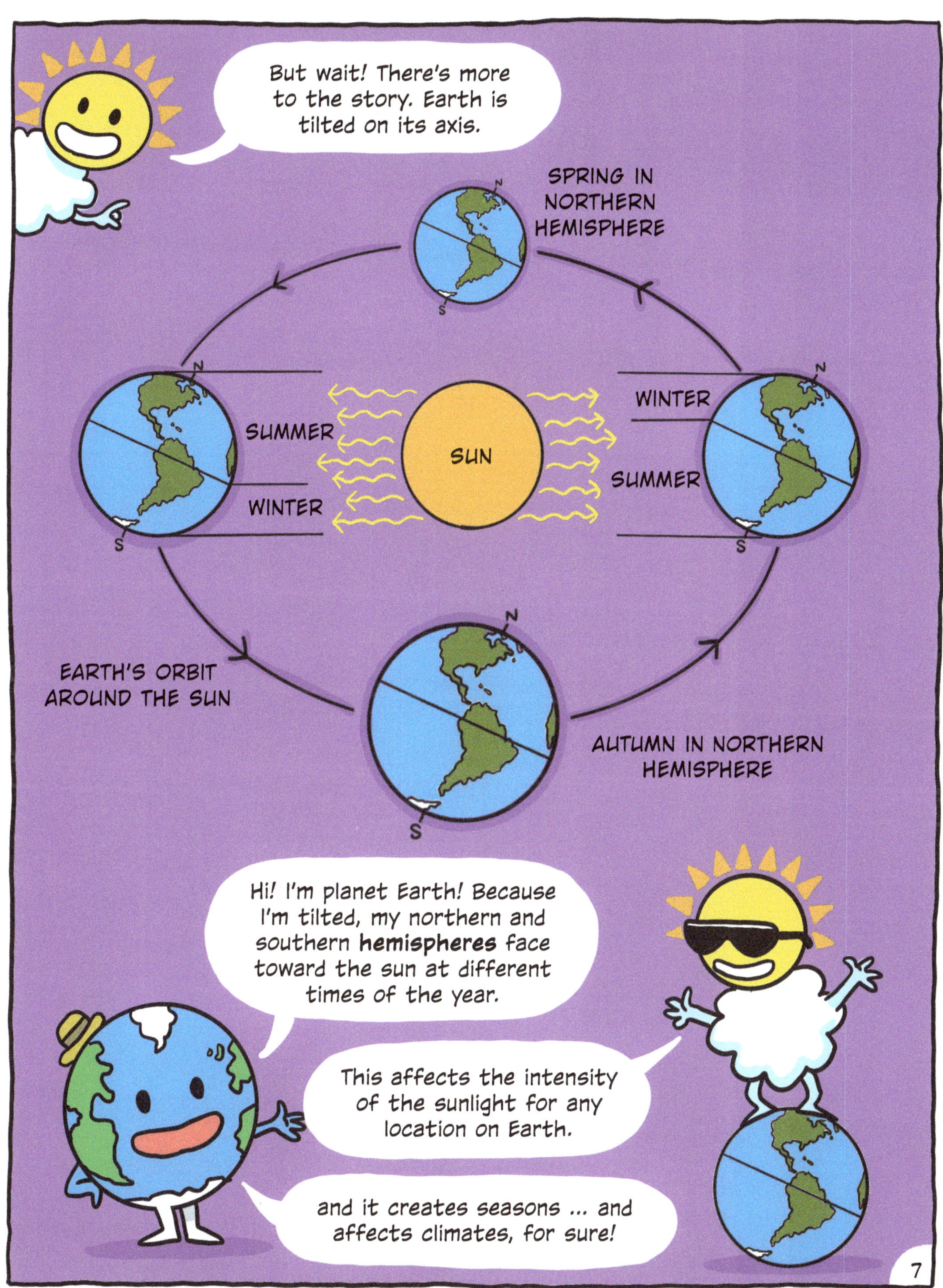

But wait! There's more to the story. Earth is tilted on its axis.
SPRING IN NORTHERN HEMISPHERE
WINTER
SUMMER
SUN
SUMMER
WINTER
EARTH'S ORBIT AROUND THE SUN
AUTUMN IN NORTHERN HEMISPHERE
Hi! I'm planet Earth! Because I'm tilted, my northern and southern **hemispheres** face toward the sun at different times of the year.
This affects the intensity of the sunlight for any location on Earth.
and it creates seasons ... and affects climates, for sure!

I think I'm a bit overdressed! In middle latitudes on Earth, temperatures change with the seasons. Seasonal highs and lows are similar each year.

The Earth's tilt also affects the length of day and night. In most places, day and night change length with the seasons. Places in the middle latitudes on Earth have warm summers with more hours of sunlight. Their winters are colder with fewer hours of daylight.
What, already?

Polar areas have very cold winters with few hours of daylight. At the North and South Poles, the sun doesn't rise at all during the winter.

Summers in polar areas have milder temperatures. There are many hours of daylight and even days in which the sun never sets.
This is impossible! I can't sleep!

The sun's rays hit the equator directly all year long. Except for at high elevations, the climate is constantly warm.

At the equator, day and night are the same length (roughly 12 hours) all year round.

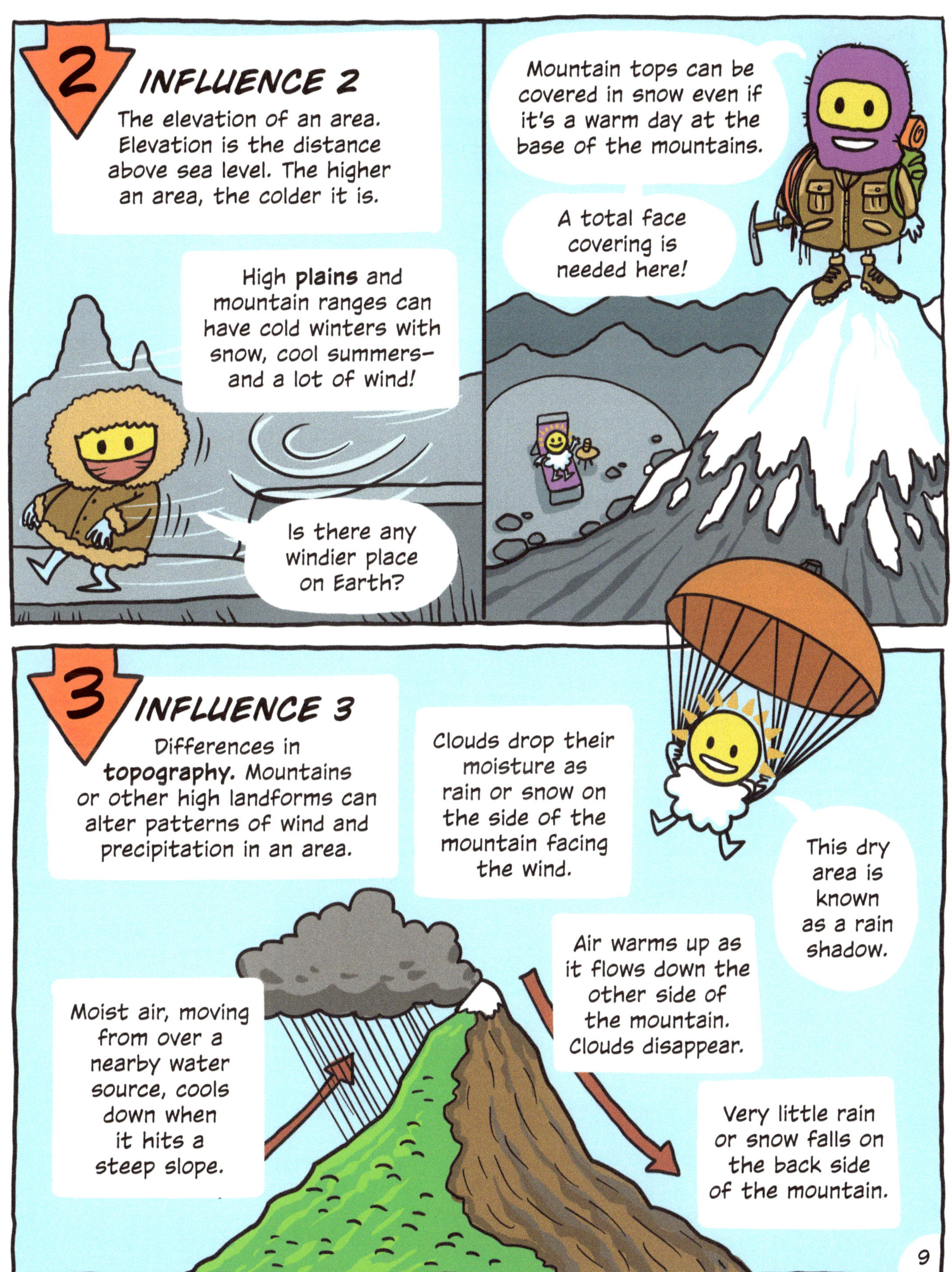

2

INFLUENCE 2
The elevation of an area. Elevation is the distance above sea level. The higher an area, the colder it is.

High **plains** and mountain ranges can have cold winters with snow, cool summers— and a lot of wind!

Is there any windier place on Earth?

Mountain tops can be covered in snow even if it's a warm day at the base of the mountains.

A total face covering is needed here!

3

INFLUENCE 3
Differences in **topography**. Mountains or other high landforms can alter patterns of wind and precipitation in an area.

Clouds drop their moisture as rain or snow on the side of the mountain facing the wind.

This dry area is known as a rain shadow.

Moist air, moving from over a nearby water source, cools down when it hits a steep slope.

Air warms up as it flows down the other side of the mountain. Clouds disappear.

Very little rain or snow falls on the back side of the mountain.

4

Large bodies of water also influence the climate nearby. Isn't that right, Ocean?
Yes! I may warm or cool the nearby land and air. The air above the oceans absorbs moisture. That can make for a wetter climate.

In summer, the temperature of a large body of water rises more slowly than the temperature on land. There's a lot of water to heat up!
Brrrr, you weren't joking!

In winter, the water in the ocean takes longer to cool down than the land does.
It's not so bad now!

Ocean currents are like huge conveyor belts that move warm or cool water around the planet.
They absorb heat around the equator and move it away to warm the waters at higher latitudes.
On to the poles with this warmer water!

The cold currents near the poles move toward the equator to cool the tropical areas.
On to the equator with this cooler water

INFLUENCE 5
5
Finally, massive bands of wind are an influence. Wind systems that blow around the planet affect the climate of the land and water over which they move. The winds are named for the direction from which they blow.
Westerlies blow from west to east. They are found between 30° and 60° north and south latitudes.
Polar winds blow from the northeast in the Arctic and the southeast in the Antarctic.
Trade winds blow toward the equator from the northeast and southeast.
Winds whip up ocean surface waves and currents.
Wind transports air, heat, and moisture around the globe.
When warm air and cold air meet, their boundary is called a front. Many wind and weather patterns are created along these fronts.
Winds create storms, such as hurricanes, tornadoes, cyclones, typhoons, and dust storms.

WHAT IS A BIOME?

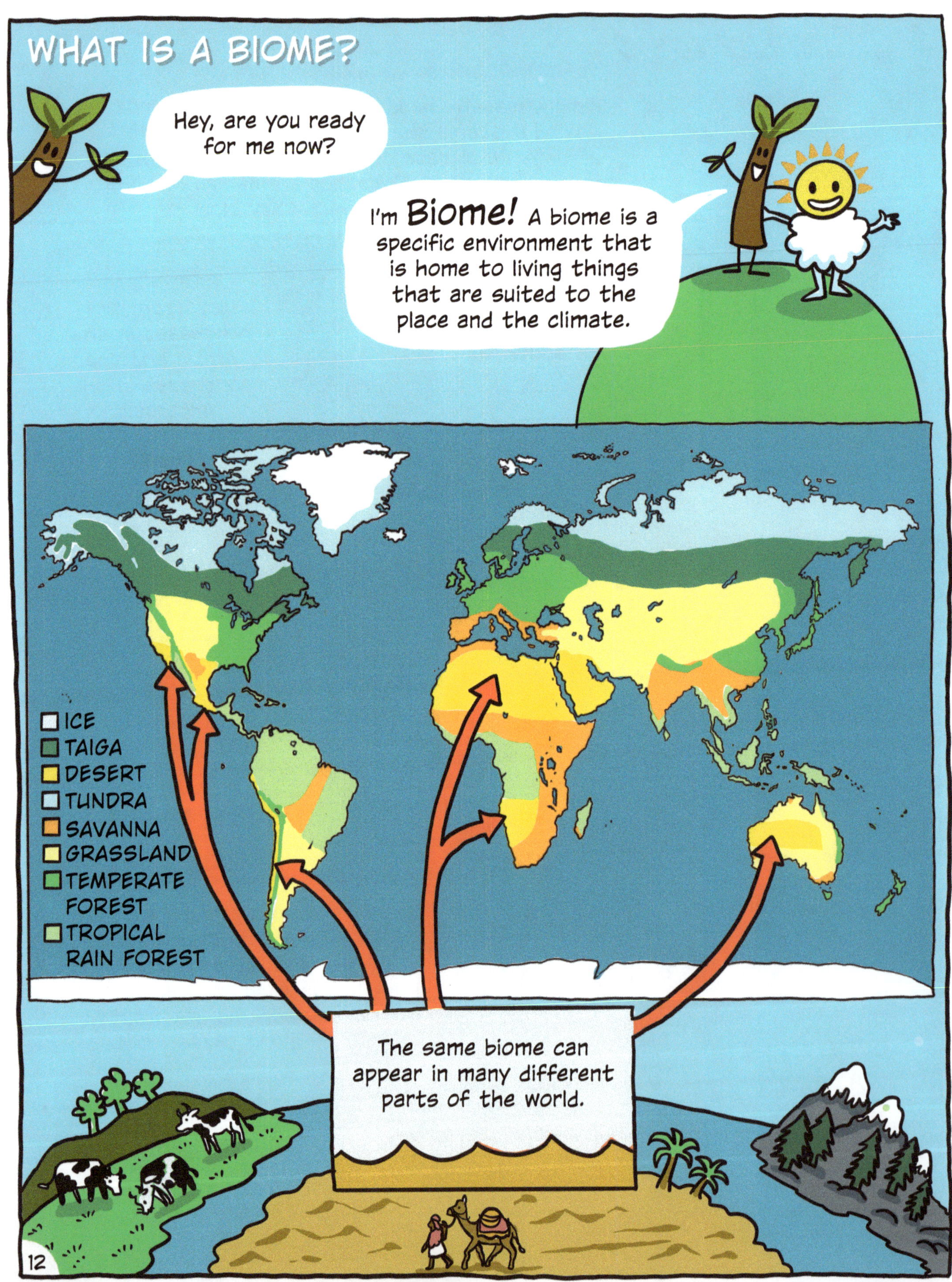

Is a biome the same as an **ecosystem**?

No, that's different. An ecosystem is all the living and nonliving things in a specific environment, such as a sand dune, and the interactions that occur among them.

There are usually many ecosystems within one biome. For example, each layer of a rain forest biome has its own ecosystem.

Wherever it is in the world, a particular biome will always have the same climate and similar species of living things. Let's take a look at some biomes now!

Welcome to the jungle! I'm starting my journey here in a tropical rain forest biome. I can see why they're called rain forests! It surely does rain a lot here!

Tropical rain forests receive at least 100 inches (254 centimeters) of rain every year. Luckily it doesn't all fall at once!

Rain forests have a tropical wet climate–a climate found only along the equator. It's hot and humid all year round.

Plants and trees grow well in the heavy rainfall, high humidity, and warm temperatures of the rain forest.

The largest tropical rain forest in the world is the Amazon rain forest in South America. It covers 2 million square miles (5.2 million square kilometers).

Rain forests are extremely **biodiverse.** This means that many different species of plants and animals live there.
Some are friendlier than others!

Just one four-square-mile area (ten square kilometers) of rain forest can contain over 700 tree species ...

... over 100 types of butterflies ...

... and 400 different bird species!

Scientists believe rain forests are home to over half of the species of plants and animals on Earth. That's millions! Biologists are finding new species every day!

The damp, dark forest floor with all its dead leaves supplies good meals for insects, worms, rodents, and such insect-eating animals as anteaters.

Farther up, the damp, warm understory is filled with flowering trees. The climate here is just right for tree frogs that need to keep their skin moist!

Up, up, up we go into the canopy—the layer of branches that is the forest's roof! Nothing blocks the sunlight or rain, so it's quite bright, but wet.

All the fruit and nut trees in the canopy make this layer home to the most animals.

What a view up here in the emergent layer! The tallest forest trees stand above the rest of the canopy.

Some small mammals up here, such as this sugar glider, can glide using flaps of skin like a parachute. Let's hitch a ride back down ...

Sadly, many rain forest biomes are being destroyed. The land is used for farming, building, or mining. In this process of **deforestation**, about 20 percent of the Amazon rain forest has been cleared.

PROTECT THE RAIN FORESTS

WHERE ARE WE SUPPOSED TO LIVE NOW?

LEAVE THE TREES ALONE!

STOP DEFORESTATION

It is important to protect this precious biome and the plants and animals that live there— before it's too late.

The rain forest isn't the only biome that is dominated by trees. Farther from the equator and the tropical regions, we find **temperate** forests.
Temperate forests grow in places with a moderate climate. All of these climates have a fair amount of rainfall and experience different seasons.
The temperatures vary from hot or warm to cool or cold, depending on the time of year. But none of the climates have extreme temperatures that hang on for months and months.

Not too hot, not too cold, just right!

The animals have **adapted** to survive different weather conditions throughout the year.
That should do it!
NUTS
NUTS
NUTS
Squirrels gather nuts in the fall and store them to eat in winter and early spring, when food is hard to find.

Many birds, such as this wood thrush, migrate in fall to spend the winter in warmer areas.
They return to the temperate forests in spring to enjoy the warm summers.
See you next year!

Some temperate forests contain mostly deciduous trees. This kind of tree loses its leaves at certain times of the year. Its leaves change color and drop off in autumn.

The tree is bare throughout the winter.

New leaf buds grow in spring.

Its leaves are fully grown by the summer.

Other temperate forests are home to mostly conifers and other evergreen trees.

These are trees with leaves like needles or scales. Conifers also have seed pods called cones.

They replace their leaves gradually, so the trees never look bare.

Judging by this snow, I'm guessing it's... winter?

Taiga biomes are full of living things adapted to withstand frigid temperatures. Many taiga animals migrate to warmer places in the coldest months.

I have thick fur to keep me warm.

My white winter coat makes it harder for **predators** to spot me in the snow ... in theory!

In the past, temperate and taiga forests covered much more land than they do today.

As early as 10,000 years ago, people began to clear areas of forest to use the land for farming.
Deforestation is a serious threat to these forests, just as it is to rain forests.

Not nearly as many areas of forest survive today. Those that do are under threat from pollution, logging, and development.

The surviving temperate and taiga forests must be protected to save these biomes from disappearing for good.
KEEP OUT

GRASSY BIOMES

When the rainy season arrives, the savanna returns to life. The grasses turn green and trees grow new leaves.

New grass shoots grow from the roots of plants that were burned in wildfires. The roots survived underground even though the rest of the plant was destroyed.

Herds of grazing animals, such as zebras and wildebeest, follow the rains around the African savanna.

These animals provide food for larger predators, such as lions and cheetahs.

The savanna is a popular place for tourists to go on a safari.

They can see an amazing show of savanna animals.

There isn't enough rainfall on the steppes for grasses to grow high. Most steppe plants are under 1 foot (30 centimeters) tall.

A prairie is a wide stretch of flat grassland with long, thick grasses and a few trees.
Prairie biomes are home to such animals as this pronghorn antelope, prairie dogs, squirrels, coyotes, and many birds and snakes.
Watch out! That's a rattlesnake!

Prairie biomes are temperate.
In these climates, rain falls in late spring and early summer. Summers can be very hot and dry. Winters are long and cold.

Prairies receive more rain than steppes (15 to 35 inches).
Finally, some rain! I'm parched!

Some prairie grasses grow taller than an adult!
Hello? Who's there?

DRY BIOMES

Deserts are the driest biomes on Earth. Very little rain falls here.

Desert biomes only get about 10 inches (25 centimeters) or less per year.

Deserts form in several ways.

Air from the equator dries and sinks over northern Africa to create the Sahara—the largest hot desert on Earth.

The Sahara Desert gets only 0 to 3 inches (0 to 7.6 centimeters) of rain a year.

The Atacama Desert in Chile is a coastal desert. Moist sea air blows fog, instead of rain, onto the land. The water droplets in fog are too small to count as rain.

Rain shadows can also cause deserts to form. Death Valley is a desert in the rain shadow of the Sierra Nevada mountains, in the western USA.

The highest ever temperature on Earth was recorded there—an unbelievable 134 °F (57 °C).

Ocean air can lose its moisture when it travels far inland.

Because of this, very little rain falls in these inland regions. And a desert biome is created!

But the animals and plants that live here all year round adapt to the heat and lack of water in different and incredible ways.

Many desert animals are **nocturnal** to avoid the daytime heat. Kangaroo rats hide away in underground burrows during the day and only come outside at night.

The large ears of the fennec fox help it to stay cool. Blood vessels in the large ears release extra heat like giant radiators to cool them down.

The saguaro cactus has roots that reach far underground to seek out water. The thick stem and waxy surface help store water and keep it from drying out.

Camels can survive without drinking water for weeks or even months. They get moisture from their food and sweat little to keep as much liquid as possible in their body.

Unlike many other biomes that are slowly disappearing due to human activity, desert biomes are expanding. This is due to a process called **desertification**.

When people cut down trees and clear plants, there is nothing left to hold the ground together.

The fertile top layers of soil are **eroded** by wind and water, leaving the land dry and bare.

This is not a good thing. These areas aren't the same as natural deserts. They don't necessarily have a desert climate. Also, the animals and plants that live in a desertified area aren't adapted for life in these conditions.

No thanks!

Planting new trees to hold the soil together is one way to prevent desertification. These trees also create new habitats and food for animals, so it's a win-win!

POLAR BIOMES

The tundra is above the tree line. This is the farthest edge of the area where trees can grow. Tundra actually means "treeless."
We can also see the tree line on a mountain.

This is because the tundra's freezing temperatures, high winds, and mostly frozen soil make it impossible for trees to grow.
I'm headed down south!

The only plants on the tundra are small shrubs and grasses. There are also many colorful lichens.

These plants grow quickly during the few weeks of milder temperatures.
Sun's out! So, grow, grow, grow!

Shrubs, grasses, and lichens provide food for tundra animals. Some of these are musk oxen, caribou, lemmings, and snow geese.
Munch, munch!

Those tundra animals provide food for predators, like Arctic wolves.
Do I smell a juicy musk ox?

The ground beneath the tundra is rich in valuable metals, oil, and coal.

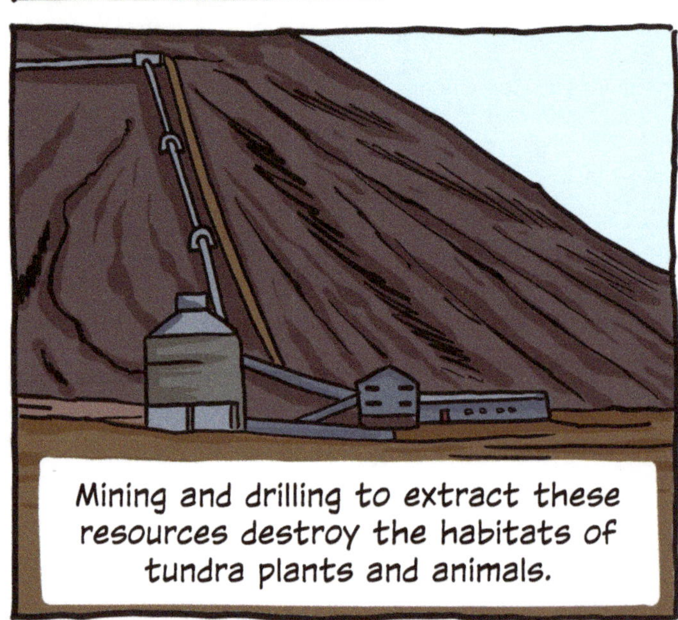

Mining and drilling to extract these resources destroy the habitats of tundra plants and animals.

Building more mines would threaten the tundra further. Passing laws to protect this biome will help save it for many years to come.
Leave the tundra alone!

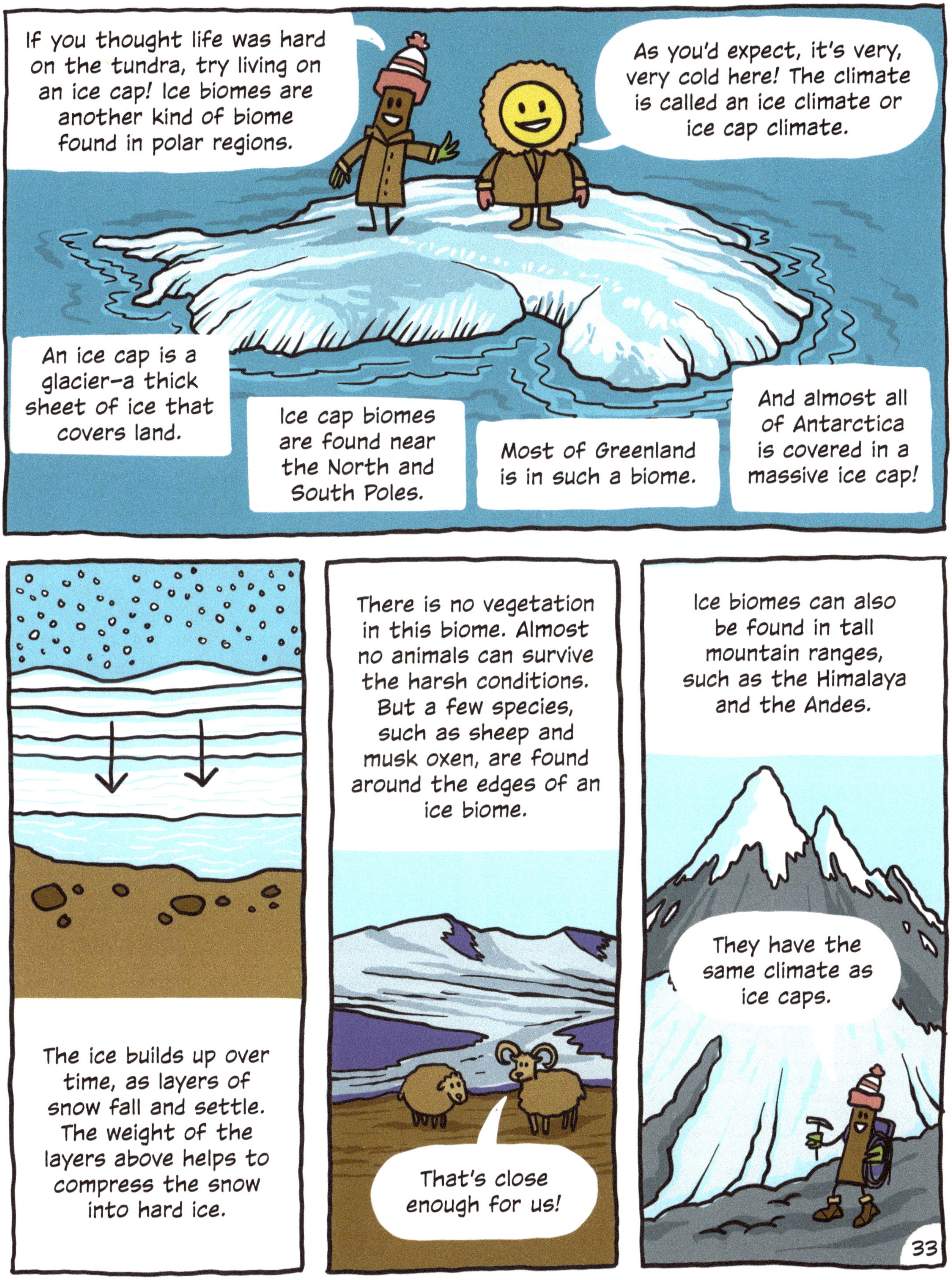

If you thought life was hard on the tundra, try living on an ice cap! Ice biomes are another kind of biome found in polar regions.

As you'd expect, it's very, very cold here! The climate is called an ice climate or ice cap climate.

An ice cap is a glacier—a thick sheet of ice that covers land.

Ice cap biomes are found near the North and South Poles.

Most of Greenland is in such a biome.

And almost all of Antarctica is covered in a massive ice cap!

The ice builds up over time, as layers of snow fall and settle. The weight of the layers above helps to compress the snow into hard ice.

There is no vegetation in this biome. Almost no animals can survive the harsh conditions. But a few species, such as sheep and musk oxen, are found around the edges of an ice biome.

Ice biomes can also be found in tall mountain ranges, such as the Himalaya and the Andes.

AQUATIC BIOMES

Most aquatic animals have a smooth, streamlined body to help them swim quickly and easily through the water.

Aquatic plants, such as algae and seaweed, need sunlight to produce food, just like plants on land. This means that they can only grow near the sunny surface of the water, as sunlight can't reach deeper areas.

The water in an estuary is a bit salty because it's a mixture of fresh water and salt water. Only certain plants and animals can survive here.

Many animals live in the kelp forest ecosystem. Sea urchins eat the kelp, and sea otters eat the sea urchins!

Fish and other animals hide from predators among the kelp.

Wow, these plants are beautiful!

Those aren't plants! These structures are built by tiny animals called coral! This whole ecosystem is known as a coral reef.

The bright, beautiful color of coral comes from microscopic algae, which grows inside the coral.

Coral reefs are found in warm, tropical oceans.

Coral reefs are very biodiverse ecosystems. Many different species live here.

Sadly, coral reefs are under threat. **Global warming** is making sea temperatures rise. Coral can't survive in hot water.

When coral dies, it also affects the other animals that live in the reef. They lose their home and their food supply.

Earth's climate has changed naturally many times throughout history. When dinosaurs were alive, most areas of Earth were warm, even the poles.

Around 11,500 years ago, the climate was much colder. Massive sheets of ice covered large areas of the planet.

However, since the mid-1800's, Earth's overall climate has become much warmer than expected. Scientists agree that this is because of such human activities as cutting down forests and burning **fossil fuels** in power stations.

When coal and oil are burned, carbon dioxide is released into the air. It gathers there with other **greenhouse gases,** such as methane, which is produced by livestock farming.

These gases trap heat from the sun close to Earth's surface. This increases the temperature on Earth. That's why they are called greenhouse gases.

The average surface temperature on Earth has increased about 2 degrees Fahrenheit (1 degree Celsius) since the mid-1800s.
This might not sound like a lot, but is enough of an increase that it has already affected many different biomes.

Ice is melting at the poles.

Extreme heat and **drought** are destroying grasslands.

If we don't stop burning fossil fuels, temperatures may be 2.0 to 11.5 degrees Fahrenheit (1.1 to 6.4 degrees Celsius) hotter by 2100.

This would have a disastrous effect on the natural world. Governments and businesses around the world must work together now to reduce global warming and protect the future of our planet.

WORDS TO KNOW

adapted able to live well in an environment because of changes that have happened to it over time.

aquatic growing or living in water.

biodiverse having many different types of animals or plants.

bog an area with soft, wet ground.

deforestation cutting down a forest or a large area of trees.

desertification when land changes into a desert.

drought a long period with little or no rain.

ecosystem all of the living things in an area and the way they affect each other.

elevation how high a place is above sea level.

equator an imaginary line around the center of Earth.

erosion the process by which Earth's materials are worn away by wind, water, gravity, or ice.

fossil fuels such fuels as coal, natural gas, and oil that are formed from the remains of ancient plants and animals.

global warming the increase in temperature on Earth.

greenhouse gas a gas, such as carbon dioxide, that traps heat in Earth's atmosphere and contributes to global warming.

hemisphere one of the two halves of Earth.

latitude the position north or south of the equator.

lichen a plant-like organism.

nocturnal active during the night.

oasis a place in the desert where there is water.

permafrost land that is permanently frozen beneath the surface.

plain a large area of flat land.

predator a hunting animal.

temperate not too hot or too cold.

topography the arrangement of physical features in an area.

tropical the region of Earth just north and south of the equator. Tropical climates are usually hot and humid.

wetland an area of land that is particularly wet.